THE SIXTH FORM POET

DEEP THOUGHTS
AND WISE WORDS

@SIXTHFORMPOET

Illustrations by Tom McLaughlin

summersdale

THE SIXTH FORM POET

Summersdale Publishers Ltd
46 West Street
Chichester
West Sussex
PO19 1RP
UK

www.summersdale.com

Printed and bound in the UK by CPI Group (UK) Ltd, Croydon, CR0 4YY
Typeset by Raspberry Creative Type

ISBN: 978-1-84953-319-5

Substantial discounts on bulk quantities of Summersdale books are available to corporations, professional associations and other organisations. For details telephone Nicky Douglas on (+44-1243-756902), fax (+44-1243-786300) or email (nicky@summersdale.com).

To Perko

Grace and Zachary B

Guess what you're getting for Christmas

From me

With love and thanks to: Mum and Fred; Jo, Rich, William, Luke and Georgie; Mr and Mrs P, Mark, Dee, Jack and Zara; Nan, Simon, Julia, Tim, Emma, Patrick and Samuel; Donna, Duncan and Joseph; Rachel and Tom.

Nolie and Bev; Tony and Holly; Chris and Shannon; Bert and Eils; Rico and Spence; Sparky and Lyds; Mat and Martine; Jamie and Kate; Paddy, Rendall and Franko.

Not forgetting G. Eric, Mary and Merv.

Finally: this book is for you, Dad. x

Hello, and thank you for picking up my book.

I've always loved jokes, so I decided to write my own. Obviously, my friends say my jokes *aren't* funny, but my mum says they're the funniest jokes ever written, clearly the work of a happy upbringing. I don't know. I look back on some of the gags here with pride; I look back on others and think I should break my own fingers. Either way, it's too late now, I just hope *you* like them.

Thank you again and enjoy.

Sixth Form Poet x

PS For more jokes, please follow me on Twitter – @sixthformpoet.

Sheryl Crow's song 'Every Day Is a Winding Road' clearly proves she's not a real crow.

Just reported a zookeeper for blatantly ignoring the Do Not Feed The Animals sign.

Becoming a musician is probably the coolest way of telling people you've lost your job.

It drives me crazy when my competitiveness gets the better of me.

My girlfriend just
bought a ruler from
Smiths. Heaven knows
I'm measurable now.

I'm visiting a model village. It's like a normal village, but with more tanning salons and fewer restaurants.

My nephew wants to be a mnemonist. I've told him to forget it, but he won't. Ever.

I'm at a Health & Safety conference. Appropriately enough, people aren't exactly falling over themselves to get in.

THE SIXTH FORM POET

When I wake up I make plans

To go out and achieve

Great things but then my bed hugs me

And begs me not to leave

When the sun shines down upon

This green and pleasant land

We celebrate by drinking beer

Until we cannot stand

'Stop blaming me for everything!!' – The Boogie

I think my eyesight's fine, but this judge disagrees. He says I need super vision.

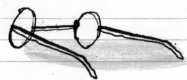

Very disappointed to learn that Radical Christianity has nothing to do with vicars on skateboards.

If you can't be with the one you love, resent the one you're with.

Every time I let my phone run out of battery, I remember why I'm no longer allowed to have pets.

I do all my own stunts, but never intentionally.

'One flew over the cuckoo's nest.' – The Queen, after taking LSD.

Marriage is Stockholm syndrome in reverse.

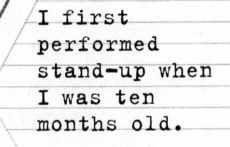

take my mother...PLEASE!

I first
performed
stand-up when
I was ten
months old.

In my ideal relationship,
neither of us would be wearing
the trousers.

'Which came first, the sturgeon
or the caviar?'
- Wealthy philosophers

My parenthesis
split up when I was at
grammar school.

THE SIXTH FORM POET

The electric blanket is the most humane method of capital punishment.

My house is certainly quieter since I persuaded the neighbours to keep mum.

Autotune is for people who enjoy singing into their airbrush.

I like to think my lack of common sense enhances all my other senses.

THE SIXTH FORM POET

STORY IDEA:

Sports team livens up games by putting a real lion into the mascot's lion outfit. Hilarity ensues.

GOOD NEWS:

Someone just told me I have a very big heart.

BAD NEWS:

It was my doctor. He says I need to change my diet immediately.

FUN FACT:

Renowned method actor Robert De Niro prepared for his role in *Little Fockers* by appearing in lots of other shit films first.

I found out my uncle was gay during a family outing.

My aunt is so posh, she prefers to be called my arenot.

Hypnotists charge an unbelievable entrance fee.

Married people fondly recall every single day of their lives.

THE SIXTH FORM POET

Never trust a kissing couple.
Their eyes are too close
together and more often than not
they're lying.

Putting all your eggs
in one basket is actually
perfectly sensible.
Carrying two baskets round the
supermarket is both awkward
and unnecessary.

My poem about tantric
sex is, at long
last, coming together
perfectly.

THE SIXTH FORM POET

My history teacher enjoyed his birthday party, but I'm still not sure he likes the present.

If she wants us to have an equal relationship, my imaginary girlfriend has a lot of making up to do.

Chefs: If your signature dish is a mess, you should resign.

Billie Jean is not my lover. She's my mixed-doubles partner.

I always sleep naked.
At least, I *did*. Then
along came Mr South
West Trains with his
silly little rulebook.

I didnt go to grammar school unfortunately

When you're a realist, the world can feel a bit flat, even though you know it isn't.

Surely it's no coincidence that Mothering Sunday is nine months after Father's Day.

I'm like a fine wine: always being drunk somewhere.

THE SIXTH FORM POET

I'm at my first meeting of Autopilot Club. We're just going through the motions now.

My plans to go ice-skating on a frozen pond have fallen through.

I was dating my hairdresser, but I've ended it. She kept talking about me behind my back.

When people ask me to bear them in mind, I imagine what they look like naked.

Is that the pitter-patter of tiny feet I can hear? Unfortunately yes. I've got head lice.

My hand is being held in a queue.

I have left the bags under my eyes unattended, in the vain hope they'll be removed and destroyed.

'Always the bridesmaid, never the bride.' - Excellent advice for a best man on the pull

THE SIXTH FORM POET

I just made my train. I preferred it when they sent them to the station ready-made.

Putting together IKEA furniture, I remind myself the instruction manual is just their opinion, and I'm equally entitled to mine.

Bakers should never put their hair in a bun.

Dads: If they're your own children it's called staying in, not babysitting.

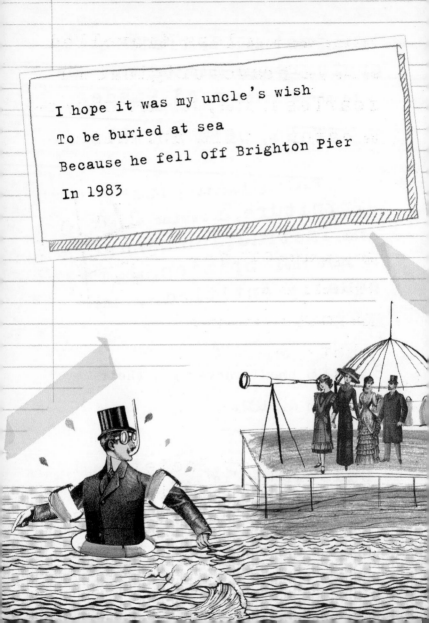

I hope it was my uncle's wish
To be buried at sea
Because he fell off Brighton Pier
In 1983

THE SIXTH FORM POET

Taking the road less travelled makes you brave, original and fearless. Also, far more likely to be eaten by wild animals.

If you describe yourself as a Marmite character, I hate you.

The Atheist Society will publish their manifesto today, barring an act of God.

THE SIXTH FORM POET

I started my new job as a clown today, and I found my feet immediately. Not surprising really, they're bright red and absolutely enormous.

Jokes about low-flying aircraft go right over my head.

Why do boxers always cuddle after a fight? If you love each other that much, why fight in the first place?

Drinking tequila is like taking the scenic route to the final verse of a Leonard Cohen song.

If life gives you lemonade, claim another small victory for evolution.

My friend just gave me a dead leg. I'm not sure whether to call the police or just hide it in the garden and hope for the best.

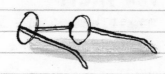

English football isn't dead, but I frequently mourn its passing.

THE SIXTH FORM POET

FUN FACT:
If you play every Beatles song
backwards, you can hear the sound of
your girlfriend closing the front
door and never coming back.

FUN FACT:
If you drown in the South Pacific, a
musical version of your life flashes
before your eyes.

FUN FACT:
The Black Eyed Peas often claim to
have just bumped into one of The
Doors.

FUN FACT:
Rock band Editors were originally
called The Editorial Assistants.

Do I have insomnia or amnesia? I was up all night thinking about it, but I've forgotten which is which.

Deep down, I knew scuba diving wasn't for me.

The most important person at Cosmetic Surgery magazine is the Features Editor.

If you can't say anything nice, say it anonymously on the Internet.

I apologise. I saw a chiropractor, not an osteopath. I stand corrected.

Even the most self-confident hostages need to be held.

My neighbour just asked if I'd take care of his little boy's hamster this weekend. I really hope that isn't a euphemism.

I wasn't quite up to joining the Mile High Club. I just felt a bit under the weather.

I don't know whether to laugh or cry, which can be incredibly awkward at funerals.

American stereotypes are like British stereotypes, but with much nicer teeth.

Having the body of a man half your age impresses no one when you're 18.

I'm hoping that what I lack in self-awareness, I more than make up for in something brilliant that I'm just not aware of yet.

I just received a spam email offering me a sex change. It begins Dear Sir/Madam.

Motivational speakers can spend entire days doing chin-ups.

A superstitious magpie can go from sorrow to mirth by simply looking in the mirror.

I wouldn't touch the banks with a bargepole. Unless, of course, my barge had run aground, in which case I'd have very little choice.

My favourite self-help
book is *Window-Dressing
For Dummies.*

I often wonder what **tomatoes** did to make the other fruits **disown** them and **force** them to live as **vegetables.**

In a **title** showdown, **Sir** Alex Ferguson will **always** beat Arsene Wenger **OBE.**

Like a **shark,** I'm deadliest when I can **smell blood.** Unless, of course, I can **see** the blood too, in which case I'll **faint.**

THE SIXTH FORM POET

Gold **earrings** are the **perfect** gift for the **au pair**.

The smell of **freshly cut** grass is a lot more **common** in **prison** than you might think.

Only **PRs** can help **ogres** make **progress**.

If you **love** someone, set them **free**. And then **spy** on them to see what they get up to when you're **not** **together**.

The older I get, the more I suspect *The Jetsons* was based on nothing more than idle guesswork.

I go out of my way to visit new places.

A barber's finest work can still end up on the cutting room floor.

People at Beachy Head quickly jump to conclusions.

THE SIXTH FORM POET

Every single person has
A dream that will never come true
Mine involves Kylie and Dannii Minogue
And a large bowl of Petits Filous

I'm completely rock and roll
I'm totally berserk
I put forks in the knife drawer
And I wear odd socks to work

The French version of Cats is a chat show.

The French couldn't organise a piste up in Abrôuerié. It doesn't snow that far north.

French protest marches are mostly non-events.

THE SIXTH FORM POET

Ironically, my Home & Contents premiums have gone through the roof.

Give a man a fish and he'll eat for a day. But only if he's a very slow eater.

I can be narcissistic, but luckily I make up for it by being incredibly handsome and charming.

I just moped around all weekend. I love mopeds.

THE SIXTH FORM POET

The spirits I drank
last night have now
come back to haunt me.

I have a recurring dream
every night at 3:33.

'You can't make an
omelette without
breaking a few rules.'
– Vegans

If you want to improve your
golf, go on a course.

I just called the vet to complain
about the excessive fees. He
put the phone down, as quickly
and humanely as possible.

'What a tangled web we weave.'
– Drunk spiders

I love make-up sex. I wonder if real sex is any better.

The worst thing about being kidnapped would probably be the embarrassing lack of facial hair when I was released.

If you're happy and you know it, clap your hands. Unless you're standing next to someone with a heart condition. Not worth the risk.

THE SIXTH FORM POET

FUN FACT:
International time zones were
first implemented in 1990, to make
sure it was always Hammer Time
somewhere in the world.

GOOD NEWS:
The girl sitting opposite me just
made firm eye contact.

BAD NEWS:
She did so by poking me in the
eye for staring at her legs.

FUN FACT:
An Eskimo's wife has 50 different
words for no.

THE SIXTH FORM POET

Some people are so self-obsessed,
like the people on this train
who don't want to hear about my day.

My cat has just one facial
                 expression and it says
'I hate you, you're not my real dad.'

I wish more TV adverts featured
sad, acoustic versions of
classic songs. That would be
nice.

Why do people get moles to conduct
undercover investigations?
Their eyesight's terrible.

THE SIXTH FORM POET

'I don't **mind** people quoting every **clever** thing I say, but a **little credit** would be nice.'
- ANONYMOUS

The real **tragedy** of *Goldilocks and the Three Bears* is that Mr and Mrs Bear, a **young married** couple, already sleep in **separate** beds.

I **love** it when people **misuse** the word *Schadenfreude*.

I've got a great joke about shoehorns. I just wish I knew how to get it into conversations.

It would be so cool if I had lots of fans.

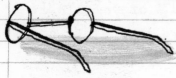

My friend and I are moving into a tree house together. I just hope we never fall out.

'I love this guy, he really speaks my language.' - Me, every time I meet a lovable Englishman.

I still
have
nightmares
about
that time
I wore
a fancy
dress to
a Fancy
Dress
party.

My boss has told so many **unfunny** jokes today, I've **forgotten** what my **real laugh** sounds like.

When people **accuse** me of being **pretentious**, I just do what my **spiritual** forefather Friedrich **Nietzsche** would do and rise above it.

I understand, you like **interfering**. What do you want, a **meddle**?

'No more Mr **Nice** Guy.' - Mr Nice Guy's **obituary.**

THE SIXTH FORM POET

If I could be any person, living or dead, I'd definitely be a living person.

I hope I live a long life. There are so many things I haven't tried and failed at yet.

Nine members of my family died because they smoked. Ten if you include my uncle, who was run over by a fire engine on his way to buy cigars.

I know, you're bulimic. I wish you'd stop bringing it up.

THE SIXTH FORM POET

The only words in my Pocket Dictionary are Keys, Wallet, Money and Fluff.

I still have nightmares about that time I gave my Eskimo friend a house-warming present.

A nudist camp will never be as entertaining as a camp nudist.

I just saw a still life exhibition at Tate Britain. I can't say I found it particularly moving.

I just had my photo taken by a tourist. I took his wallet, just to even things up.

I'm only a social drinker. I'm just very, very sociable.

The older I get, the more I question my history teacher's idea that we should be naked in class to maximise the benefit of wearing clothes outside.

I hope the blood on my plate is from the steak, not the hand-cut chips.

THE SIXTH FORM POET

Diamonds are a girl's best friend

While man's best friend's a hound

A clearer case that girls know best

Will surely not be found

There is nothing English people

Love more than the rain

We have to pay for most things which

Allow us to complain

I was stunned when I found out that tasers work.

How could people be expected to complete the eleven-plus, when they didn't even finish the question?

The only TV channel in Heaven is Sky Living +1.

I spent the weekend converting to Buddhism. There's an entire lifetime I will be getting back.

When people say they can't get out of bed, they're usually lying.

I hate clichés, but other people love them. Swings and roundabouts, I guess.

Sean Connery's hair is always in a mesh first thing in the morning.

I just dropped a jar of mayonnaise on my foot. The last thing the wound needs is dressing.

THE SIXTH FORM POET

I just made a mental note. It makes no sense whatsoever.

Just had an idea. If the economy continues to struggle, perhaps we could try and commercialise Christmas in some way.

I am sitting on a train. I should probably climb back inside before we reach a tunnel.

I always hit the ground running, so I'm giving up running.

FUN FACT:

Bumblebees are not the lovable buffoons their name suggests. They're highly-trained pollen thieves and violent if provoked.

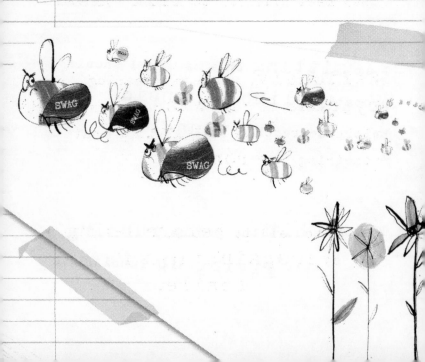

THE SIXTH FORM POET

I'm at the opera. We're applauding after every movement. This must be what potty-training is like.

The Gingerbread Man is the perfect story for teaching children that if they run away from home, everyone they meet will try to kill them.

Seriously, can a man wearing pyjamas not buy wine at 9am without everyone assuming that something is wrong?

I've said it before and I'll say it again: I think I'm going senile.

Busy doctors should treat themselves at the weekend.

I have given up wearing my smoking jacket, thanks largely to the patches on the elbows.

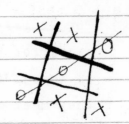

I love meditation. It gives me the chance to pause, reflect and ask myself important questions, such as 'Do I look as silly as I feel?'

Drinking chasers will catch up with you eventually.

THE SIXTH FORM POET

I found Lord Lucan and Shergar

In a deep freeze in my shed

I will be rich if the microwave can

Somehow bring them both back from the

dead

If I ask you if you would

Like sugar in your tea

And you say 'No, I'm sweet enough'

You can't be friends with me

THE SIXTH FORM POET

When sports reporters describe slightly frosty pitches as Arctic conditions, I begin to suspect they've never actually been to the Arctic.

'You snooze, you lose.' - Insomniac propaganda

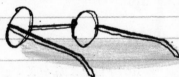

Of Britain's many theme parks, PC World has by far the best wheelchair access.

Restaurant critics must get fed up with their jobs.

THE SIXTH FORM POET

My older brother calls me his disappointing sequel.

The weather outside is biblical, by which I mean fascinating to some, but of no interest to others.

I've been told to work smarter, not harder. I'm halfway there.

Since you ask, my last servant died in a freak yachting accident. Thanks for bringing it up, you insensitive prick.

The Waste Land is a littery masterpiece.

THE SIXTH FORM POET

The older I get, the more I suspect my dad was lying when he told me eating bananas would help me see around corners.

'Maybe it's Maybelline' sounds like a very subtle disclaimer.

I always get a bit punchy when I drink rum.

My friend just said a film appeals to the child in him. As you can imagine, I'm quite upset that my friend once ate a child.

THE SIXTH FORM POET

I'm just a boy, standing in front of a girl, asking her to accept that rules like 'Ladies first' simply don't exist on the Tube during rush hour.

People use the term 'snooze-fest' as a criticism, but I think a week-long festival of snoozing would be awesome.

What is my sexual persuasion? Well, a nice meal and a couple of bottles of wine usually does the trick.

Having amnesia's given me a real boost. I genuinely feel like my entire life is ahead of me.

THE SIXTH FORM POET

Sorry ladies, my **ventriloquist's** dummy is already **spoken** for.

'I never mix **business** with **pleasure.**'
— Someone who **hates** their job

Maybe I'm not **imaginative** enough, but if I had a **time machine**, I think I'd just fast-forward to **bedtime.**

If you're **happy** and you **know** it, your childhood **memoir** will **never** get published.

THE SIXTH FORM POET

When chefs have insomnia

Instead of counting sheep

They much prefer to count lamb chops

And quickly fall asleep

My aunt and uncle were together

Thirty years or more

But then bizarrely he was found

In bed with John next door

THE SIXTH FORM POET

I just bought *Groundhog Day* on Amazon. Surprised there wasn't a 'same-day delivery' option.

The Shoplifter of the Year competition is now open. No purchase necessary.

If I told you I was shrinking, would you think less of me?

Fool me once, shame on you. Fool me twice, shame on you again. And stop picking on me, I'm clearly an idiot.

THE SIXTH FORM POET

I always feel a bit **negative**
after a **takeaway.**

My uncle won a **lifetime's
supply** of **chocolate** once.
He ate the **whole lot** in
one afternoon. And then **died,**
obviously.

In an **unrelated**
incident, my **sister**
and **I** were adopted.

I'm **worried** my life is a Choose
Your Own **Adventure** story,
in which I make a series of **bad
decisions** and eventually get
eaten by dinosaurs.

THE SIXTH FORM POET

Terrible parenting, a cross-dressing wolf and a brutal axe murder. Little Red Riding Hood really is the perfect story for young children.

'Cross-Dressing Wolf' Slept With My Grandma.

THE SIXTH FORM POET

I'd hate to be famous, mostly
because I want to go on
Deal or No Deal and celebrities
have to give their winnings to
charity.

My friend said he'd give me £100
if I did a bungee jump. I wasn't
falling for that.

I'd be a lot happier about my test
results coming back negative
if it hadn't been a personality
test.

The first half of Lolita's
hilarious.

THE SIXTH FORM POET

Imagine my disappointment when I realised my IQ score wasn't out of 100.

Meeting your heroes will always end in disappointment. Especially if you're rummaging through their dustbins at the time.

I'm a man of simple needs. It's the stuff I *want* that would give psychoanalysts nightmares.

My boss just said he's going to get me 'an extra pair of hands'. I'm going to look *ridiculous*.

FUN FACT:

Anne Boleyn and Catherine Howard
were neck and neck in Henry VIII's
affections.

FUN FACT:

Ancient Romans called 40 'XL'
because that was the age when
they had to start wearing bigger
clothes.

GOOD NEWS:

Girls think I have a magical power.

BAD NEWS:

It's invisibility.

FUN FACT:

Everybody knows it was William Goldman
who said 'Nobody knows anything.'

KNOCK KNOCK!!

Who's the—

JEREMY PAXMAN!!

Jeremy Pax—

I ASK THE QUESTIONS!!!

Everyone starts their
weekend with a wee.

I just completed my first novel.
I enjoyed it so much, I might even
try reading another one soon.

THE SIXTH FORM POET

I love the sun, but it's so high
and mighty. Thinks the whole
world revolves around it.

Grammar Nazis are notoriously
anti-semantic.

Most people would rather their
office caught fire than endure
the small talk caused by weekly
fire drills.

I live every day as if it's my
last. Under a blanket with my
eyes closed.

THE SIXTH FORM POET

Sixth Form Poet's last girlfriend **left** him because of the **third person** in their relationship.

Getting some very **odd** looks at work today. I was always told 'dress for the job you **want**, not the one you **have**'. I want to be an **astronaut.**

You **are** what you **eat,** and I wish I'd **never eaten** that **bumbling** idiot.

Cleanliness is next to **godliness** on my list of things I don't quite have the **energy** for on **Sunday** mornings.

A Freudian slip is
when you say one
thing, but mean
amother.

actually, I'm Jung at hea

My **failed** career in
Minimalist Art left me
seriously overdrawn.

There were **ten** in the
bed and the little
one said **Rollover!**
Rollover! He'd won the
Euromillions and was
celebrating with nine
prostitutes.

(University Challenge +
Newsnight) x CBeebies =
Question Time

My last girlfriend left me after
she caught me wearing her favourite
dress. I said 'Please don't go, I can
change.'

'I'd never cut off my nose to spite my face. I'd only do it if I really wanted to eat a carrot.'
– A snowman

Of all the different blood groups, Type Os make the most spelling mistakes.

You scratch my back and I'll scratch yours? No, I'm English. You scratch my back and I'll tell you to stop being overfamiliar.

Every time I try to fight my insecurities, my lack of confidence holds me back.

Johnny Rotten was born on the same day that A. A. Milne died. Possibly not the conclusive proof that reincarnation exists I was hoping for.

I always feel a bit flat after a nice evening out.

Never be afraid of the obvious. Unless you're being mugged, obviously.

My **favourite** thing about being English is having to say 'Sorry, excuse me, thank you' every time some **idiot** walks into me.

Never judge a **book** by its low-budget, **badly miscast** TV adaptation.

'Fail to **prepare**, prepare to **fail**.' You're not **listening**, are you? I never prepare for anything.

THE SIXTH FORM POET

The saddest Christmas story is

The one about the boy

Who had 10,000 batteries

But not a single toy

Merry
x mas

THE SIXTH FORM POET

I love the thrill of the chase.
Well, I did before I began chasing my
dream of being a fully-qualified
accountant.

My friends have entered me in an
Innuendo Contest.

Jersey is a close-knit community.

I've worked my socks off to
overcome my nerves, but I'm
getting cold feet now.

THE SIXTH FORM POET

I'm such a determined character. Once I get the bit between my teeth, nothing can stop me from getting a toothpick.

You can tell a lot about a person from their favourite book. Stealing their phone and reading their texts also works.

Kate and Pippa Middleton are like strawberries and cream. They're both nice, but the two of them together would be delicious.

THE SIXTH FORM POET

Yawning is suggestive, apparently, but my date just yawned and it didn't look very suggestive to me.

My archaeology career is in ruins.

If someone shakes their fist at me, I quickly out-do them by shaking all over.

Girlfriends are like passwords: if you've shared them with your friends, you should probably get a new one.

THE SIXTH FORM POET

FUN FACT:
Only one word in the English
language is ever pronounced
correctly, and that word is
correctly.

FUN FACT:
Racehorses always slow down if
they see a police horse standing
by the side of the course.

TOP TIP:
If you're drunk, steady yourself by
placing a beermat under your foot,
as you would with a wobbly table.

FUN FACT:
Most skunks are teetotal. Some enjoy
the occasional beer, but for most
the association with drunkenness is
completely unfair.

THE SIXTH FORM POET

I've been reading *Osteopathy* magazine for years. I have lots of **back** issues.

Pancake jokes are for **tossers.**

I think the **Rorschach** family next door look **lovely**, but my **friend** thinks they look like **church-burning** Satanists.

My cat is **stuck-up** in a tree. People are **beneath** her.

THE SIXTH FORM POET

Unsliced Bread never quite came to terms with his younger brother's success.

The seven-year-old me would be furious if he knew how little time I now spend in tree houses.

Middle-aged cheese makers insist a few Gruyères make them look distinguished.

The less I think about reverse psychology, the more I think I should give it a try.

When I see a Goodfella's pizza in the freezer, I assume it's there because it betrayed the other pizzas.

THE SIXTH FORM POET

I just made my hamster a strong coffee. I don't want him falling asleep at the wheel.

'Tinker, Tailor, Soldier, Spy.' - Just four of the million lies on my CV.

I'm a man trapped outside a woman's body.

Judging by his tendency to wear distinctive clothes in densely populated areas, I'm starting to think Wally wants to get caught.

I just saw a notice on a pub door saying Guide Dogs Only. Possibly the most exclusive pub ever.

A bear drops an e and turns into a bar.

BEAR: Er... just a water, please.

BARMAN: Why the big pause?

BEAR: I love you, man.

I remember when my ex-girlfriends were all over me. Now they're all over me.

Triathlons are
three-legged races
for grown-ups.

THE SIXTH FORM POET

Marrying your **best friend** sounds great, **except** my best friend's an **idiot**. And he's got a girlfriend.

Rude people? No thank you.

I just bought **crack** for the **fourth** day in a row. Starting to **worry** I might be a shopaholic.

'Love means **never** having to say you're **sorry**.' - No girl, ever.

I will never eat my own words. I'm too full of myself.

Neil Diamond is the perfect accompaniment to a marriage proposal.

I exercise religiously. Once at Christmas, again at Easter, not very much in between.

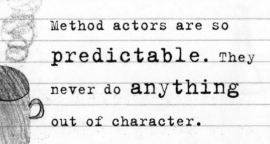

Method actors are so predictable. They never do anything out of character.

THE SIXTH FORM POET

The smallest thing can turn a morning person into a moaning person.

Judging by his reaction to losing his mobile phone signal, the man sitting opposite me would be ill-prepared to lose an actual human being.

Every person has a story to tell, which is why I never talk to people.

You had me at 'Hello, I've been drinking since lunchtime.'

THE SIXTH FORM POET

Life is easy to begin with

But then adolescence

After which your life is mostly

Spent in convalescence

If I were God and I liked jazz

I know what I would do

I'd paint the sky a very cool

Miles Davis kind of blue

THE SIXTH FORM POET

Relationships can be **transformed** in Paris hotels.

I'm a **singer**, which gives me **terrible** migraines.

Saying to a friend 'Your baby's so **cute**, are you **sure** it's yours?' is a **subtle** and **amusing** way of suggesting his **wife** sleeps around.

When you're as good at **levitation** as I am, it's **hard** to keep your **feet** on the ground.

THE SIXTH FORM POET

In a school of fish, red herrings
are notorious for
distracting their classmates.

Rainbows are such a beautiful
reminder of Richard of York's
brutal and ultimately
pointless death.

Queen bees often come out in hives.

I am thinking the
unthinkable. HOW IS THAT EVEN
POSSIBLE?!!

THE SIXTH FORM POET

My youthful exuberance is on the slide. Weeeeeeeeeeeeeeeeeee! I love slides.

When people are badly let down, they feel just a little bit deflated.

I should confront my shyness, but I never will. I hate confrontation.

Disaster, I forgot to clean my teeth. I've been told to eat a packet of mince, but that's just making things worse.

Hostages are bound to agree with their captors.

Girls' names are like passwords: get it wrong, access denied.

My boss says we need a perfect day today, so I'm off to drink sangria in the park, then I'm off to the zoo. Later, a movie too, and then home.

'And the rest is history.'
– Me, after having a rest.

THE SIXTH FORM POET

FOOTBALL CLUBS:

If a rival club says they'll only
accept 'silly money' for a player,
offer them chocolate coins.

TOP TIP:

Always treat new work colleagues like
old friends. At least until you're
100% certain they're not the secret
millionaire.

OPTIMISM:

Where there's a will, there's a way.

PESSIMISM:

Where there's a will, someone died.

STORY IDEA:

Internet fraudsters hack into my bank
account and make a series of shrewd
investments. Hilarity ensues.

THE SIXTH FORM POET

I have recently downgraded my plans for this time next year from 'millionaire' to 'not homeless'.

An optimist has a condom in his wallet, a realist has a photo of his wife. I'm a pessimist: I have a photo of a condom.

I'm so badly in debt, my bank now sends me a monthly understatement.

THE SIXTH FORM POET

My polo shirt is in mint condition, despite having a hole in the middle.

Not knowing the difference between patronising and condescending is nothing to worry your silly little self about.

Blind auctions leave lots to the imagination.

I just found a message in a bottle. It said 'Keep drinking me and I'll teach you to dance.' I love wine.

THE SIXTH FORM POET

The Stranglers did all their best work using the same three cords.

My friends say I spend too much time in front of the mirror. I disagree, but I will look into it immediately.

Rocking horses are kept in unstables.

Dear Man Wearing Yellow Trousers In Public. You're wearing yellow trousers. In public. Just thought you should know. You're welcome.

THE SIXTH FORM POET

I've lived with my head in the clouds so long, my hair now has a silver lining.

THE SIXTH FORM POET

Criminals: Pretend you're
in an episode of *Scooby-Doo*
by confessing and fully
explaining your motives the
moment you're accused.

An OD will always spell the end
of your childhood.

I love the irony of 'irony' being
the most frequently misused
word in the English language.

It must be so hard to prove
Viagra works.

When people **accuse** me of being **delusional**, I quickly arrange to have them **killed** by my close **friends** in the Sicilian Mafia.

It's a source of **great embarrassment** that Punk's **full** name is Punctilious.

Depressed actors join **Negative** Equity.

Poker's like a séance: you sit around a **table** holding **hands**, and one guy **profits** from **everyone** else's loss.

A stranger is just a friend I haven't let down yet.

Tapeworms are bookworms with reading difficulties.

If I heard the pot calling the kettle black, I'd definitely stop smoking the pot.

Managers: Some employees need a carrot, others a stick. Play safe and give your staff carrot sticks.

THE SIXTH FORM POET

I'm seeing a Harley Street therapist for help with my kleptomania, and I've already taken something valuable from every session.

Everybody remembers where they were when they found out that JFK had been assassinated. I was in a History class.

Girlfriends are like buses: you wait for ages and I like the bendy ones best.

THE SIXTH FORM POET

My birthday suit will last me a lifetime

That much is never in doubt

I wear it in the bath of course

But never wear it out

J-Lo and I had a mucky affair

Then I went camping with Sonny and Cher

Osama Bin Laden came back from the dead

I must stop eating cheese before bed

THE SIXTH FORM POET

A modern remake of *The Boy Who Cried Wolf* would feature a Health & Safety officer obsessed with fire drills.

Every time I agree to Terms & Conditions without reading them first, I picture Keith Moon giving me a big thumbs up.

Spin doctors never call a spade a spade. They call it a ground-breaking innovation.

THE SIXTH FORM POET

I will literally eat my own head
the next time I see someone misuse
a word when trying to be clever.

'Baby, You can Drive My Car'
is my favourite song about
irresponsible parenting.

'I'm Spartacus!'
– Spartacus's twin brother,
caught shoplifting.

A horse walks into a bar.
BARMAN: Why the long face?
HORSE: Because you tell that joke
every time I come here.

THE SIXTH FORM POET

I never run away from my problems, mostly because my biggest problem is laziness.

Mondays: Be more popular by rebranding as Sunday +1.

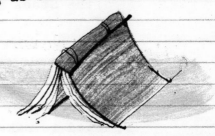

I keep my inappropriate jokes about mental health in a special case.

THE SIXTH FORM POET

STORY IDEA:

Boy meets girl. Girl texts boy sweet
message. Boy texts girl photo of his
penis. Girl texts boy photo of *her*
penis. Hilarity ensues.

FUN FACT:

The OXO Tower has excellent views of
the Stock Exchange.

BREAKING NEWS:

The Leaning Tower of Pisa
expected to make a decision
shortly.

FUN FACT:

Ancient Romans could get eleven
in the back of a taxi.

I'm terrible at phone sex.
Apparently I sound like I'm having
a stroke.

My nephew is being sent to see
a child psychologist. We'd
rather he saw a grown-up,
but they're so much more expensive.

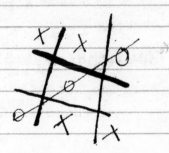

I'm afraid my spiritual home
is being repossessed.

I spent today at a Spar. Not as relaxing as I'd been led to believe.

Identity theft is the sincerest form of flattery.

I just found a pigeon lying dead by the road. Now looking for the Flight Data Recorder to work out what happened.

People who spend a first date lying often spend the second date stood-up.

I owe my parents everyt
will pay them back tomo
after which I'm never playing
poker with them again. Pair of
cheats.

Winning an Oscar is nice,
but for most actors it's the
taking parts that counts.

The five stages of Monday:
Denial, Anger, Bargaining,
Depression, Wine.

I just shot the messenger.
Now wishing someone had
told me not to.

Making fun of
dyslexic barmen is
just taking peach
shots.

In the case of the negligent
babysitter, charges were dropped.

THE SIXTH FORM POET

Everyone loves Monopoly,
but walk into a Park Lane
hotel wearing nothing
but a top hat and, trust
me, nobody laughs.

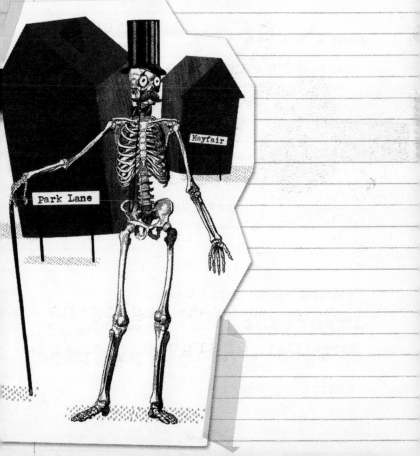

THE SIXTH FORM POET

There's a **very** thin line between a **misunderstood genius** and a **pretentious** idiot **nobody likes.**

When I'm lying on my deathbed, my one big regret will be that I'm lying on my deathbed.

'I just get completely wasted every day.'

– Time

Nothing says 'your call is **important** to us, please stay on the **line**' quite like a **pan pipe** version of *Imagine.*

THE SIXTH FORM POET

Life **begins** at 40, which is why so **many** people in their forties **behave** like children.

Sadly, I **lost** both my **parents** when I was **eleven**. Not been to Hampton Court **Maze** since.

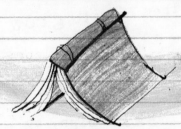

If writers took the 'write what you know' rule **seriously**, most new **novels** would be called *Constantly* **Distracted** *By The* **Internet**.

THE SIXTH FORM POET

Do you ever make yourself laugh out loud? I do, every time my boss tells me an unfunny joke.

My teeth chatter amongst themselves one minute, fall out over a toffee the next. Some of them need to grow up.

I got bored holding a Golf Sale sign, so I handed in my notice.

It takes 43 muscles to frown, and yet it's still not an Olympic event. Ridiculous.

My heart is just like a spare room

Where not many people have stayed

However, recently I had a guest

You should see the mess that she made

I always say dyslexia

Is not such a bad thing

For every time I see a sign

I feel the urge to sing

If women really want to be treated as equals, they need to stop being so much smarter than men.

I'm paranoid and needy: I think people are talking about me, but not as much as I'd like.

My favourite thing about the lottery is that the odds on you winning the jackpot barely change if you forget to buy a ticket.

If you have a funny sneeze, the world laughs with you, not ATCHOOO!!!

THE SIXTH FORM POET

I'm a Sixth Form Poet,
but fiddle with me and I
become a Hot Firm Sexpot.

Acknowledgements

Abbie Headon

Adam Hess

Adam Kay

Adam Postans

Ade Bradley

Aidan Marrin

Al Murray

Alan Buckley

Alan Stoob

Alex Winters

Amro Gebreel

Andrea Mann

Andrew Cottier

Annabel Giles

Archie Bland

Arpi Arayan

Barry Welch

Ben Brougham

Ben Cameron

Ben Horsley

Benedict Farse

Bob Nelmes

Boothby Graffoe

Cameron Addicott

Caroline Walsh

Cassandra Donovan

Charlotte Ross

Chris Addison

Chris Hancock

Chris Hibble

Chris Twidale

Ciaran Murray

Colm Tobin

Conor Burke

Daisy Batchen

Dan Brennan

Dan Rebellato

Dan Warren

Daniel Cluedont

Daniel Kramer

Daniel Mayhew

Danny McNamara

Dave Bromage

Dave Gorman

David Allan

David Harris

David Stokes

David Whitley

David Willis

Dean Wattam

Delia Ryan

Derek Morecambe

Duncan Powell

Edward Philips

Ella Bell

Elliott Clarkson

Emily Bryce Williams

Erik Kennedy

Fenner Pearson

Frank Brinkley

Frankie McGinty

G. Rhydian Morgan

Gary Bainbridge

Glenny Rodge

Graham Linehan

Heidi Smith

Henry James Baulch

Ian Botterill

Ian Leak

Ian Martin

Ian Power

Jack Seale

Jake Lambert

James Farrell

James Martin

Jay Richardson

Jim Sheridan

Joe Martin

John Brennan

John Roe

John Self

Jonathan Shipley
Jonathan Wood
Josh Hara
Josie George
Julian Dutton
June Walmsley
Keiley Roberts
Keith Ryan
Ken Armstrong
Kerry Smith
Kirsten Shaw
Laura Sparling
Lewis Heriz
Liam P. Copas
Lils Rebellato
Lily Wilde
Lise Sand
Liz Buckley
Liz Stowe
Lizzie Logs
Mark Templeton
Martin Carr
Martin Shovel
Martyn Cotterill
Mat Horne
Matt Leys
Matt Thorogood
Matt Whatsit
Melody Metcalf

Michael Moran
Michael Spicer
Miles Orru
Moose Allain
Musa Okwonga
Neil Dutton
Neil Mawer
Nick Beaton
Nick Harvey
Nick Motown
Nooruddean Choudry
October Jones
Omar Shah
Parvez Anwar
Patrick Brennan
Paul Bassett Davies
Paul Ellerker
Paul Groom
Peter Serafinowicz
Quintin Forbes
Rachel Hedgehog
Rhys James
Richard Herring
Richard Kirby
Richard Neville
Richard Orme
Richard Stoker
Rob Hale
Rob Richardson

Rodger Nash
Roger Quimbly
Russell Morton
Scarlet Musgrave
Shappi Khorsandi
Sharon Taylor
Shaun Fendley
Shaun Usher
Simon Blackwell
Simon Caney
Simon Evans
Simon Guerrero
Simon Ricketts
Simon Whiteside
Soulla Tantouri Eriksen
Stephen Grant
Stu Kershaw
Suzanne Waters
Tara Flynn
Tim Burgess
Tom Carney
Tom Doorley
Tom Freestone
Tom Jamieson
Tom Milsom
Victoria Hellon
Vivienne Clore
Zola Affley

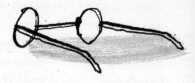

If you're interested in finding out more about our humour
books, follow us on Twitter: @SummersdaleLOL

www.summersdale.com